Secret Societies

A discussion of their character and claims

**David MacDill,
Jonathan Blanchard,
And Edward Beecher**

Secret Societies: A discussion of their character and claims

For information and contact visit our website at:
IndoEuropeanPublishing.com

The present edition is a revised version of an earlier publication of this work, produced in the current edition with completely new, easy to read format, and is set and proofread by Alfred Aghajanian for Indo-European Publishing.

Cover Design by Indo-European Design Team

ISBN: 978-1-60444-273-1

IndoEuropean
Publishing.com
Los Angeles, CA, USA

CONTENTS

PART I

SECRET SOCIETIES: A TREATISE

CHAPTER I

Their Antiquity

1. Secret associations are of very ancient origin. They existed among the ancient Egyptians, Hindoos, Grecians, Romans, and probably among nearly all the pagan nations of antiquity. This fact, however is neither proof of their utility nor of their harmlessness. Slavery, despotism, cruelty, drunken falsehood, and all sorts of sins and crimes have been practiced from time immemorial, but are none the less to be reprobated on that account.

2. The facts that these associations had no existence among the Israelites, who, alone of all the ancient nations, enjoyed the light of Divine revelation, and that they originated and flourished among the heathen, who were vain in their imaginations; whose foolish heart was darkened, and whom God gave up to uncleanness through the lusts of their own hearts (Rom. i: 21-24), is a presumptive proof that their nature and tendency are evil. We do not claim that all the institutions among God's ancient people were right and good; nor that every institution among the heathen was sinful and injurious; still, that which was so popular among those whom the Bible declares to have been filled with all unrighteousness; that which was so pleasing to men whom God had given over to a reprobate mind and to vile

affections (Rom. i: 26-28); that which made a part of the worship which the ignorant heathen offered up to their unclean gods, and which was unknown among God's chosen people, is certainly a thing to be viewed with suspicion. A thing of so bad origin and so bad accompaniments we should be very slow to approve. The fact that many good men see no evil in secret societies, and that many good men have been and are members of them, is more than counterbalanced by the fact that many good men very decidedly disapprove of them, and that, from time immemorial, men of vile affections and reprobate minds, men whose inclinations and consciences were perverted by heathenish ignorance and error, and by a corrupt and abominable religion, have been very fond of them.

3. Doubtless the authors and conductors of the ancient *mysteries* made high pretensions, just as do the modern advocates of secret societies. Perhaps the original design of the ancient mysteries was to civilize mankind and promote religion; that is, pagan superstition. But whatever may have been the *design* of the authors of them, it is certain that they became schools of superstition and vice. Their pernicious character and influence were so manifest that the ancient Christian writers almost universally exclaimed against them. (Leland's Chr. Rev., p. 223.) Bishop Warburton, who, in his "Divine Legation," maintains that the ancient mysteries were originally pure, declares that they "became abominably abused, and that in Cicero's time the terms mysteries and abominations were almost synonymous." The cause of their corruption, this eminent writer declares to be the *secrecy* with which they were performed. He says: "We can assign no surer cause of the

horrid abuses and corruptions of the mysteries than the *season* in which they were represented, and the profound silence in which they were buried. Night gave opportunity to wicked men to attempt evil actions, and the secrecy encouragement to repeat them." (Leland's Chr. Rev., p. 194.) It seems to have been of these ancient secret associations that the inspired Apostle said, "*It is a shame even to speak of those things which are done in secret.*" (Eph. v: 12.)

4. In view of these facts, the antiquity of secret societies is no argument in their favor; yet it is no uncommon thing to find their members tracing their origin back to the heathenish mysteries of the ancient Egyptians, Hindoos, or Grecians. (See Webb's Freemason's Monitor, p. 39.) Since the ancient mysteries were so impure and abominable, those who boast of their affinity with them must be classed with them of whom the Apostle says, "*Their glory is in their shame*" (Phil, iii: 19.)

CHAPTER II

Their Secrecy

1. One of the objectionable features of all the associations of which we are writing is their secrecy. We do not say that secrecy is what is called an *evil or sin in itself.* Secrecy may sometimes be right and even necessary. There are family secrets and secrets of State. Sometimes legislatures and church courts hold secret sessions. It is admitted that secrecy in such cases may be right; but this does not prove that secrecy is *always* right. The cases above-mentioned are exceptional in their character. For instance, a family may very properly keep some things secret; but were a family to act on the principle of secrecy, they would justly be condemned, and would arouse suspicions in the minds of all who know them. Were a family to endeavor to conceal every thing that is said and done by the fireside; were they to invent signs, and grips, and passwords for the purpose of concealment; were they to admit no one under their roof without exacting a solemn oath or promise that nothing seen or heard shall be made known, every one would say there is something wrong. So, too, if a church court would always sit in secret; were none but members at any time admitted; were all the members bound by solemn promises or oaths to keep the proceedings secret, and were they to employ signs, grips, and passwords, and to hold up horrid

threats, in order to secure concealment, such a church court would lose the confidence of all men whose esteem is of any value. Such studious and habitual concealment would damage the reputation of any family or church court in the estimation of all sensible people. The same result would follow in case a Legislature would endeavor, as a general thing, to conceal its proceedings. As to State secrets, they generally pertain to what is called diplomacy; and even in straightforward, manly diplomacy there is generally no effort at concealment. In our own country, Congress very often asks the President for information in regard to the negotiations and correspondence of the Executive Department with foreign governments, and almost always the whole correspondence asked for is laid before Congress and published to the country. It is very seldom that the President answers the call with a declaration that the public welfare requires the correspondence to be kept secret. Besides this, the concealment is only temporary. It is never supposed that the secrecy must be perpetual. It is true that many diplomatists—perhaps nearly all the diplomatists of Europe—do endeavor to cover up their doings from the light of day. It is also true that the secrecy and deceit of diplomatists have made diplomacy a corrupt thing. Diplomacy is regarded by many as but another name for duplicity. Talleyrand, the prince of diplomatists, said "the design of language is to conceal one's thoughts." This terse sentence gives a correct idea of the practice of secret negotiators. With regard, then, to State secrets, we remark that real statesmen do not endeavor to cover up their doings in the dark, and that the practices of diplomatists, and the reputation they have for duplicity, are not such as should encourage individuals or associations to endeavor to conceal their proceedings. We see nothing in the fact that there may be secrets of State to justify studied and habitual secrecy either in individuals or associations.

2. The impropriety of habitual concealment may be further illustrated. An individual who endeavors to conceal the business in which he is engaged, or the place and mode of carrying it on, exposes himself to the suspicion of his fellow-men. People lose confidence in him. They feel that he is not a safe man. They at once suspect that there is something wrong. They do not ask or expect him to make all his business affairs public. They are willing that he should say nothing about many of his business operations. But habitual secrecy, constant concealment, unwillingness to tell either friend or foe what business he follows, or to speak of his business operations, will cause any man to be regarded as destitute of common honesty. This fact shows that, in the common judgment of men, constant concealment is suspicious and wrong. Wherever it is practiced, men expect the development of some unworthy purpose.

We regard secrecy just like homicide and other actions that in general are very criminal. To take human life, as a general thing, is a very great crime; but it is right to kill a man in self-defense, and to take the life of a murderer as a punishment for his crime. The habitual concealment of one's actions is wrong, but it may be right at particular times and for special reasons. It is not a dreadfully wicked thing, like the causeless taking of human life, and may be justifiable much oftener and for less weighty reasons. Still habitual secrecy, or secrecy, except at particular times and for special reasons, is, according to the common judgment of men, suspicious and unjustifiable. Now, with secret societies secrecy is the general rule. They practice constant concealment. At all times and on all occasions must the members keep their proceedings secret. If an individual would thus studiously endeavor to conceal his actions; were he to throw the veil of secrecy over his business operations, refusing to speak to any of his fellow-men concerning them, he would justly expose himself to suspicion. His fellow-men would lose all confidence in his integrity. If habitual secrecy on the part of an individual, in regard to business matters, is confessedly suspicious and wrong, it must be so, also, on the part of associations of men. There is less excuse, indeed, for concealment on the part of a number of men banded together than on the part of an individual. An individual working in the dark may do much mischief, but an association thus working can do much more. All those considerations which forbid individuals to shroud their actions in secrecy and darkness, and require them to be open, frank, and straightforward in their course, apply with equal or greater force to associations.

3. In the case of secret societies, the reasons for concealment set the impropriety of it in a still stronger light. So far from there being any necessity or special reason to justify habitual secrecy in their case, we believe the very *design* of their secrecy to be improper and sinful. We present the following quotation from a book of high authority among those for whose benefit it was specially intended:

"If the secrets of Masonry are replete with such advantages to mankind, it may be asked, Why are they not divulged for the general good of society? To which it may be answered, were the privileges of Masonry to be

8

indiscriminately bestowed, the design of the institution would be subverted, and, being familiar, like many other important matters, would soon lose their value and sink into disregard."—*Webb's Freemason's Monitor, p. 21.*

The same author intimates that the secrecy of Masonry is designed to take advantage of "a weakness of human nature." He admits that Masonry would soon sink into disregard if its affairs were generally known. Although this remark is made with special reference to the giddy and unthinking, yet it is certainly not the contempt of such persons which Masons fear. They would not care for the contempt of the giddy and unthinking, if they could retain the esteem of the thoughtful and wise. The real reason, then, for concealing the doings of Masons in their lodges, is to recommend things which, if generally known, would be regarded with contempt. The design of concealment in the case of other secret associations, we understand to be the same. The following is an extract from an address delivered at the national celebration of the fortieth anniversary of Odd-fellowship, in New York, April 26, 1859, and published by the Grand Lodge of the United States:

"But even if we do resort to the aid of the mysterious, to render our meetings attractive, or as a stimulant to applications for membership, surely this results, in no injury to society or individuals."—*Proceedings of Grand Lodge of United States,* 1859, *Ap., p.* 10.

Here, again, it is pretty plainly hinted that the design of secrecy in the case of Odd-fellowship, is to invest it with unreal attractions, or, at least, with attractions which it would not possess, were the veil of concealment withdrawn. Here, again, as in Masonry, it is virtually admitted that secrecy is designed to take advantage of "a weakness in human nature," and to recommend things which, if not invested with the attractions which secrecy throws around them, would sink into contempt.

Doubtless the design of concealment in the case of other secret associations is the same. We are not aware that Good-fellows, Good Templars, Sons of Temperance, and other similar associations, have any better reason for working, like moles, in the dark than Masons and Odd-fellows. There is, then, as it respects secret societies, no necessity for concealment—nothing to justify it. The real motive for it is itself improper and sinful.

4. That the concealment of actions and principles, either by individuals or associations, is inconsistent with the teachings of the Bible, is, we think, easily shown. Thus our Savior, on his trial, declared: "*I spake openly to the world; I ever taught in the synagogue, whither the Jews always resort; and in secret have I said nothing.*" (John xviii: 20.) An association which claims to be laboring in behalf of true principles, and for the moral and intellectual improvement of men, and yet conceals its operations under the impenetrable veil of secrecy, is certainly practicing in direct opposition to the example and teaching of the Son of God.

Again: The concealment of our actions is condemned in the words of the Most High, as recorded by the prophet: "*Woe unto them that seek deep to hide their counsel from the Lord, and their works are in the dark; and they say, Who seeth us? and who knoweth us?*" (Is. xxix: 15.) Those on whom a divine curse is thus pronounced are described as endeavoring to *hide their works in the dark*. This description applies, most assuredly, to those associations which meet only at night, and in rooms with darkened windows, and which require their members solemnly to promise or swear that they will never make known their proceedings.

Again: The inspired apostle incidentally condemns secret societies in denouncing the sins prevalent in his own day: "*And have no fellowship with the unfruitful works of darkness, but rather reprove them; for it is a shame to speak of those things that are done of them in secret.*" (Eph. v: 11, 12.) It is not without reason that commentators understand the shameful things done in secret, of which the apostle speaks, to be the "mysteries" of the "secret societies" which prevailed among the ancient heathen. They maintained religious rites and ceremonies in honor of their imaginary deities, just as most modern "secret societies" make a profane use of the word and worship of God in their parades and initiations. He says it would be a shame to speak of the rites performed by the heathen in their secret associations in honor of Bacchus and Venus, the god of wine and the goddess of lust, and of their other abominable deities. But whether the apostle refers to the Eleusinian, Samothracian, and other pagan mysteries, or not, the *principle of secrecy* comes in for a share of his condemnation.

The concealment practiced by "secret societies" is inconsistent, also, with such declarations of the Bible as the following: "*For every one that doeth evil hateth the light, neither cometh to the light, lest his deeds should be reproved. But he that doeth truth cometh to the light, that his deeds may be made manifest that they are wrought in God.*"(John iii: 20, 21.) "*Let your light so shine before men that they may see your good*

11

works, and glorify your Father which is in heaven." These are the words of our Savior, and they certainly condemn the concealment practiced by secret associations, and all the means employed for that purpose—their signs, grips, and passwords; their shunning the light of day; their secret gatherings in the night, and in rooms with darkened windows; the terrible oaths and solemn promises with which they bind their members to perpetual secrecy; the disgraceful punishments which they threaten to inflict on any member who will expose their secret doings—all these things are inconsistent with the spirit, if not the very letter, of the commands of our Savior quoted above.

5. Besides, if the doings of these associations, in there secret meetings, are *good,* then it is in the violation of the express command of our Savior to keep them concealed; for he tells us to let others see our good works. In case their doings are bad, it is, perhaps, no violation of Christ's command to keep them hid; but, most certainly, such things ought not to be done at all. So far as the moral character of secret societies is concerned, it matters not whether the transactions which they so studiously conceal are good or bad, sinless or wicked. If such transactions are good, the Savior commands that they be made known; if they are improper and sinful, he commands us to have no fellowship with them. In either case secret associations are to be condemned as practicing contrary to the teachings of the Bible.

Hence, we conclude that the concealment so studiously maintained and rigidly enforced by the associations whose moral character we are considering is condemned both by the common judgment of men and by the Word of God.

12

CHAPTER III

Their Oaths and Promises

1. Another serious objection to secret associations is the profanation by them of the oath of God. We regard such profanation as the natural result of their secrecy. When associations of men endeavor to keep secret their operations from generation to generation, they will not be willing to trust to the honor and honesty of their members. A simple promise of secrecy will not be deemed sufficient. Oaths or promises, with dreadful penalties, will very likely be required of all those who are admitted as members. Secret societies may, perhaps, exist without such oaths and promises. If the members of an association are few in number, or if the publication of its secrets would not be regarded as very injurious to its interests, perhaps a simple promise of secrecy will be regarded as sufficient; but whenever an association endeavors to secure a numerous membership, and regards a disclosure of its secrets as likely to damage its reputation or hinder its success, something more than a simple promise of secrecy will very likely be required at the initiation of members. Accordingly, some secret associations, it is known, do employ awful sanctions in order to secure concealment. Even when the members of a secret order claim that they are not bound to secrecy by oath, but only by a simple

promise, it will, perhaps, be found on examination that that promise is, in reality, an oath. An appeal to God or to heaven, whether made expressly or impliedly, in attestation of the truth of a promise or declaration, is an oath. Such an appeal may not be regarded as an oath in our civil courts, the violator of which would incur the pains and penalties of perjury; yet certainly it is an oath according to the teachings of the Bible. Our Savior teaches that to swear by the temple, is to swear by God who dwelleth therein; and that to swear by heaven, is to swear by the throne of God, and by him that sitteth thereon. (Matt. xx: 23.) We find, also, that the words, "As the Lord liveth," is to be regarded as an oath. King David is repeatedly said to have sworn, when he used this form of expression, in attestation of his sincerity. (1 Sam. xx: 3; 1 Kings i: 29.) An appeal to God, whether direct or indirect, in attestation of the truth of a declaration or promise, is an oath. As we have already said, a secret association may exist without an oath. But we are not sure that any does. Odd-fellows have declared that they have no initiatory oath. In the address published by the Grand Lodge of the United States, referred to before, the following declaration is made: "No oath, as was once supposed, is administered to the candidate." (App. to Proceedings of Grand Lodge, 1859, p. 10.) Yet Grosch, in his Odd-fellows' Manual, speaks of an "appeal to heaven" in the initiation, at least, into one of the degrees. (P. 306.) Perhaps the contradiction arises from a difference of opinion in regard to what it takes to constitute an oath, or, perhaps, from the fact that an oath is required in initiations into some degrees, but not in others. However this may be, we know that some secret societies have initiatory oaths, and that nearly all administer what, in the sight of God, is an oath, though they may not so view it themselves. Nor do we see any reason to discredit the declaration of Grosch that the candidate "appeals to heaven."

2. Now, the taking of an initiatory oath is, to say the very least of it, of doubtful propriety. Every one who does so swears by the living God that he will forever keep secret things about which he knows nothing. The secrets of the association are not imparted to him until after he has sworn that he will not reveal them. He is kept ignorant of them until the "brethren" are assured by his appeal to heaven that they can trust him. Now, the inspired apostle lays down the principle that a man sins when he does any thing about the propriety of which he is in doubt. He declares that the eating of meats was in itself a matter of indifference, but that if any man esteem any thing unclean, to him it is unclean. He then makes the following declaration: "But he that doubteth is damned if he eat, because he eateth not of faith; for whatsoever is not of faith is sin." (Rom. xiv: 22, 23.) According to this most emphatic declaration, we must have faith and confidence that what we do is right, else we are blameworthy. We sin whenever we do any thing which is, according to our own judgment, of doubtful propriety. The man who is initiated into an oath-bound society, swears that he will keep secret things about which he knows nothing—things which, for aught he knows, ought not to be kept secret. If the apostle condemned, in most emphatic language, the man who would do so trivial a thing as eat meat without assuring himself of the lawfulness of his doing so, what would he have said had the practice existed in his day of swearing by the God of heaven in regard to matters that are altogether unknown? To say the very least, such swearing is

altogether inconsistent with that caution and conscientiousness which the Scriptures enjoin. The apostle also condemns the conduct of those who "*understand neither what they say nor whereof they affirm*" (1 Tim. i: 7.) Does not his condemnation fall on those who know not about what they swear, nor whereof they appeal to heaven?

3. There is another objection to taking an initiatory oath. We are expressly forbidden to take God's name in vain. To pronounce God's name without a good reason for doing so is to take it in vain. Certainly, to swear by the name of the living God demands an important occasion. To make an appeal to the God of heaven on some trifling occasion is a profanation of his oath and name. If the secrets of Masonry, Odd-fellowship, Good Templars, and similar associations, are unimportant, their oaths, appeals to heaven, and solemn promises made in the presence of God are profane and sinful. Perhaps their boasted secrets are only signs, grips, pass-words, and absurd rites of initiation. To swear by the name of the Lord about things of this kind is certainly a violation of the third commandment. The candidate does not *know* that the secrets about to be disclosed to him are of any importance, and he runs the risk of using God's name and oath about light and trivial things. He must be uncertain whether there is any thing of importance in hand at the time of swearing, and how can he escape the disapproval of God, since the inspired Paul declares that the doubtful eater of meat is damned? (Rom. xiv: 23.)

4. We have already adverted to the fact that concealment is resorted to in order to take advantage of "a weakness in human nature," and to recommend things which, if known

16

generally, would be disregarded. Is it right to use the name and oath of God for the accomplishment of such purposes? Is it right to use the name and oath of God in order to take advantage of "a weakness in human nature," and to invest with fictitious charms things which, if seen in the clear light of day, would be regarded with indifference or contempt? The taking of oaths for such purposes, and under such circumstances will generally be avoided by those who give good heed to the command, "Thou shalt not take the name of the Lord thy God in vain; for the Lord will not hold him guiltless that taketh his name in vain."

5. While we do not claim that there is any passage of Scripture which expressly declares the initiatory oaths under consideration to be profane and sinful, at the same time there are many passages which require us to beware how and when we swear:

"But above all things, my brethren, swear not, neither by heaven, neither by the earth, neither by any other oath; but let your yea be yea, and your nay, nay, lest ye fall into condemnation." (James v: 12.) Does not this command condemn those who swear to keep secret they know not what, and to fulfill obligations which devolve upon them as members of an association, before they know fully what that association is, or what those obligations are? Should not every one consider himself admonished not to swear such an oath lest he fall into condemnation? Again: Our Savior says, "Swear not at all; neither by heaven, for it is God's throne; nor by the earth, for it is his footstool; neither by Jerusalem, for it is the city of the great king. Neither shalt thou swear by thy head, because thou canst not make one hair white or black; but let your communication be yea, yea, nay, nay; for

whatsoever is more than these, cometh of evil." These words were spoken in condemnation of those who employed oaths frequently and on improper occasions. They should make every one hesitate in regard to swearing, in any form, on his initiation into an order the obligations and operations of which have not yet been revealed to him. Once more: "*Be not rash with thy mouth, and let not thine heart be hasty to utter any thing before God, for God is in heaven and thou upon earth; therefore, let thy words be few.*" (Eccl. v: 2.) Is it not a rash thing to bind one's self by the oath of God to keep secret things as yet unknown, or to bind one's self to conform to unknown regulations and usages? In view of these declarations of the Word of God, it certainly would be well to avoid taking such oaths as generally are required of the members of secret associations at their initiation.

6. The *promise* required of candidates at their initiation, whether there be an oath or not, is also, at least in many cases, improper and sinful. For instance, the "candidate for the mysteries of Masonry," previous to initiation, must make the declaration that he "will cheerfully conform to all the ancient established usages and customs of the fraternity." (Webb's Freemason's Monitor, p. 34.) Grosch, in his Odd-fellows' Manual, directs the candidate at his initiation as follows: "Give yourself passively to your guides, to lead you whithersoever they will." (P. 91.) Again, in regard to initiation into a certain degree, he says: "The candidate for this degree should be firm and decided in his answers to all questions asked him, and patient in all required of him," etc. (P. 279.) In the form of application for membership, as laid down by Grosch, the applicant promises as follows:

"If admitted, I promise obedience to the usages and laws of the Order and of the Lodge." (P. 378.)

These declarations, by reliable authors, plainly show that both in Masonry and Odd-fellowship obligations are laid on members of which, at the time, they are ignorant. Candidates for Masonry must promise to conform, yes, "cheerfully conform to all the ancient established usages and customs of the fraternity." The application for membership in the association of Odd-fellows must be accompanied by a promise of obedience to the usages and laws both of the whole Order and of the lodge in which membership is sought. No man has a right to make such a promise until he has carefully examined the usages, and customs, and laws referred to. While he is ignorant of them, he does not know but some of them or all of them may be morally wrong. Before the candidate has been initiated, he has not had an opportunity of acquainting himself with all the laws, usages, and customs which he promises to obey. Is not such a promise condemned by the divine injunction, "Be not rash with thy mouth?" Is not the man who promises to obey regulations, customs, and usages before he knows fully what they are as blameworthy as the doubtful eater of meats, who, the inspired apostle tells us, is damned for doing what he is not confident is right? The candidate for initiation into Odd-fellowship must "give himself passively to his guides." Such demands indicate the spirit which secret associations require of their members. They must surrender the exercise of their own judgment, and permit themselves to be blindly led by others. No man has a right thus to surrender himself passively to the guidance of others. Every man is bound to act according to his own judgment and conscience. Before a man promises to obey any human regulations, or to conform to any usage or custom, he is bound to know what that regulation, usage, or custom is, and to see that it is morally right. To do otherwise is to sin against conscience and the law of God.

7. Besides this, the promise to "preserve mysteries inviolate," made before they have been made known to the promiser, is condemned by sound morality. He may have heard the declaration of others that there is nothing wrong in "the mysteries," but this is not sufficient to justify him. A man is bound to exercise his own reason and conscience in regard to all questions of morality.

No man has a right, at any time, to lay aside his reason and conscience and allow himself to be "guided passively" by others. Every man is bound to see and decide for himself in every case of duty and morals. We should not let the church of Christ even decide for us in such matters, much less some association, composed, it may be, of infidels, Mormons, Jews, Mohammedans, and all sorts of men except atheists. (See pages 37, 31.) A band of such men may have secrets very immoral in character, and which it would be a violation of God's law to preserve inviolate. To promise beforehand that any "mysteries" which they may see fit to enact and practice shall be forever concealed, is to trifle with conscience and morality. It is useless to plead that a member can withdraw as soon as he discovers any thing wrong in the regulations and usages which he is required to obey. Every one who joins such an association as those under consideration must make up his mind to do so before he knows what "the mysteries" are, and he must promise (either with or without an oath) that he will preserve them inviolate before "the brethren" will intrust them to him. The possibility of dissolving his connection with the association afterward does not exonerate him of promising to do he knows not what—of laying aside his own conscience and reason, and yielding himself "passively" to others. The promise of secrecy and of obedience to unknown regulations and customs, required at the initiation of candidates into such associations as we are considering, is, therefore, a step in the dark. It involves the assuming of an obligation to do what *may be* morally wrong, and is, therefore, inconsistent with the teachings of the Word of God and the principles of sound morality.

CHAPTER IV

Their Profaneness

1. Another evil connected with secrecy, as maintained by the associations the character of which is now under consideration, is the profane use of sacred things in ceremonies, celebrations, and processions. This evil has, perhaps, no *necessary* connection with secrecy, but has generally in *fact*. The "secret societies" of antiquity dealt largely in religious ceremonies. It is the frequent boast of Masons, Odd-fellows, and others, that their associations correspond to those of ancient times. There is, indeed, a correspondence between them in the use of religious rites. Those of ancient times employed the rites of heathenish superstition; those of modern times are, perhaps, as objectionable on account of their prostituting the religion of Christ. The holy Bible, the word of the living God, is used by Masons as a mere emblem, like the square and compass. The pot of incense, the holy tabernacle, the ark of the covenant, the holy miter, and the holy breastplate are also employed as emblems, along with the lambskin and the sword pointing to a naked heart. At the opening of lodges and during initiations, passages of Scripture are read as a mere ceremony, or as a charge to the members in regard to their duty as Masons. Thus a perverse use of holy Scripture is made in the application of it to matters to which it has no

reference whatever. (Freemason's Monitor, pp. 92, 19-181). Even the great Jehovah is represented in some of their ceremonies by symbols. His all-seeing eye is represented by the image of a human eye. (Freemason's Monitor, pp. 85, 290.) Masonry also profanes the name and titles of God. God alone is to be worshiped; he alone should be addressed as the *Most Worshipful Being*. But Masonry requires the use of such language as follows: "The Most Worshipful Grand Master," and "The Most Worshipful Grand Lodge." God alone is Almighty, but Masons have their "Thrice Illustrious and Grand Puissant," and their "Thrice Potent Grand Master." God alone is perfect, but Masons have a "Grand Lodge of Perfection" and a "Grand Elect Perfect and Sublime Mason." (Monitor, pp. 187, 219; Monitor of Free and Accepted Rite, pp. 52.) Christ is the great High Priest, and Aaron and his successors were his representatives, but Masons have a "High Priest," a "*Grand* High Priest," yea, a "*Most Excellent* Grand High Priest." At the installation of this so-called High Priest, various passages of Scripture treating of the priesthood of Melchisedec and of Christ are used. (Webb's Monitor, pp. 178-181, 187.)

We regard these high-sounding titles as ridiculous, and as well calculated to excite derision and scorn; but we do not now treat of them in that regard. We call attention, at present, to the emblems and titles used by Masons as profane. God did not intend his holy Word, and the Tabernacle, and the Ark of the Covenant, and the Breastplate, to be used as the symbols of Masonry. These and other holy things were intended only for holy purposes. To use them as the Masons do is to pervert and profane them. The visible representation of the all-seeing

eye of God is certainly a species of idolatry, and is
forbidden by the second commandment. Such, also, are the
triangles, declared to be "a beautiful emblem of the eternal
Jehovah." (Monitor, p. 290.) The Israelites, of course, did
not understand that the Divine Being was really like their
golden calf; they considered it a symbol of Deity. How
much better is it to assimilate God to a *triangle* than to a
calf? The difference is just this: the latter idea is more gross
than the former. The sin of idolatry—that is, of
representing God under a visible figure—is involved in
both cases. The profaneness of the titles mentioned above
must at once be evident to every reverent, considerate
mind. They are such as in the Bible are ascribed only to
God and to Christ. Indeed, Masons give more exalted titles
to their sham priest than the Scriptures employ to describe
the character and office of the great High Priest who is
"made higher than the heavens." If this is not profane, we
are at a loss to know what can be profane.

2. The Odd-fellows in profanation of holy things go about
as far as the Masons. They employ "the brazen serpent,"
"the budded rod of Aaron," "the Ark of the Covenant," "the
breastplate for the high priest," and other holy things as
emblems of their order, along with, "the shining sun," "the
half moon," etc. They have their "Most Worthy Grand
Master," and their "Most Excellent Grand High Priest," and
other officers designated by titles which should be given to
God and Christ alone. Indeed, as it respects emblems and
titles, Masonry seems to be the example which other secret
associations have followed. In regard to the profanation of
holy things, the difference between most of the secret
associations in our land is one merely of degree. This
profanation of the word, name, and titles of God is

certainly sinful in itself, and very injurious in its effects. What kind of ideas of God, and Christ, and heaven must persons have who conceive and think of God under the figure of three triangles; of Christ and his priesthood as symbolized by "the Most Excellent Grand High Priest," officiating amid the tomfooleries of Masonry and Odd-fellowship; and of heaven as a Grand Lodge-room. What ideas of the Divine Majesty and Glory must they have who are accustomed to give to the officers of a secret association, and to men who are, perhaps, destitute of faith and holiness, and who may be Jews, Turks, or infidels, as grand titles as the Scriptures give to the God of heaven and the Savior of the world. Besides it is very improper and sinful to give to mere men the titles and glory which are due to God alone. We learn that it was precisely for this sin that the Divine displeasure was visited upon king Herod. On a certain occasion having put on his royal apparel, he sat on his throne and made a public oration. The people who heard him shouted and said, *"It is the voice of a God and not of a man; and immediately the angel of the Lord smote him, because he gave not God the glory; and he was eaten of worms, and gave up the ghost."* (Acts xii: 23.) It was for the same spirit of self-glorification that the king of Babylon was punished with madness and disgrace. Nebuchadnezzar walked in his palace, and said: "Is not this great Babylon, which I have built for the house of my kingdom by the might of my power, and for the honor of my majesty?" The same hour he was driven from men, and did eat grass as oxen; and his body was wet with the dew of heaven, till his hairs were grown like eagles' feathers, and his nails like birds' claws. (Dan. iv: 30-33.)

2.

Another objectionable feature of many secret societies is, that they profane the *worship* of God. They claim (at least those which seem to embrace the most numerous membership) to be, in some sense, religious associations. They maintain forms of worship; their rituals contain prayers to be used at initiations, installations, funerals, consecrations, etc. They receive into membership, as we shall afterward see, almost all sorts of men except atheists. Being composed of Jews, Turks, Mohammedans, Mormons, and infidels, as well as of believers in Christianity, they endeavor to establish such forms as will be acceptable to their mongrel and motley membership. Hence their prayers and other forms of worship are such as may be consistently used by the irreligious and by infidels, and only by them. We do not say that no Christian prayers are offered up in Masonic lodges. No doubt some godly men, as chaplains, offer up extempore prayers in the name of Christ; but such prayers are not Masonic. They are not authorized by the Masonic ritual; they are contrary to the spirit if not to the express regulations of Masonry. Any member would have a right to object to them, and his objections would have to be sustained. The only prayers which Masonry does authorize, and can consistently authorize, are Christless—infidel prayers and services. The proof of this declaration can be found in every Masonic manual. (See Webb's Monitor, pp. 36, 80, 189, and Carson's Monitor, of the Ancient and Accepted Rite, pp. 47, 61, 95, 99.) In all the prayers thus presented, the name of Christ is excluded; it is excluded even from the prayers to be offered at the installation of the "Most Excellent Grand High Priest." (Webb's Mon., pp. 183, 189.) The idea of human guilt is, also, almost entirely excluded from these prayers; the idea of pardon through the atonement of Christ is never once presented in them. In the prayer to be used at the funeral of a "Past Master," it is declared that admission unto God's "everlasting kingdom is the just reward of a pious and virtuous life." Every true Christian, on reflection, must see that such prayers are an insult to the Almighty. They are just such as infidels and all objectors of Christ may offer.

The prayers of the society of Odd-fellows are equally objectionable. In respect to the character of their religious services, they are to be classed with the Masons. Odd-fellowship knows no God but the god of the infidel; it recognizes the Creator of the Universe and the Father of men, but not the Father of our Lord and Savior Jesus Christ. The name of Christ has no more a place in the religion of Odd-fellowship, according to its principles and regulations, than in a heathen temple or an infidel club-room. It is quite likely that sometimes chaplains, officiating in the lodge-room, pray in the name of Christ; but a Turk, according to the principles and regulations of Odd-fellowship, would have just as much right to pray in the name of Mohammed, or a Mormon in the name of Joe Smith. These are facts which, we presume, all acquainted with the forms and ceremonies in use among Odd-fellows will admit. Grosch, in his Manual, makes the following declaration: "The descendants of Abraham, the divers followers of Jesus, the Pariahs of the stricter sects, here gather round the same altar as one family, manifesting no differences of creed or worship; and discord and contention are forgotten in works of humanity and peace." (Pp. 285, 286.) This declaration has reference, of course, to *all* the members of the associations—believers in Christianity, Jews, Mohammedans, Indians, Hindoos, and infidels. How do they manage to worship so lovingly together in the lodge-room? Our author asserts that they "leave their prejudices at the door." Of course their forms of worship embody no "prejudices." The thing is managed in this way: Whatever is peculiar to Judaism is excluded from the ritual and worship of Odd-fellows; whatever is peculiar to Hindooism is excluded; whatever is peculiar to Mohammedanism is excluded; whatever is peculiar to Christianity is excluded; whatever is peculiar to any form of religion is excluded. Only so much as is held in common by Jews, Hindoos, Mohammedans, and Christians is allowed a place in the ritual and worship of Odd-fellows. But how much is held in common by these various classes? After every thing peculiar to each class has been thrown overboard, how much is left? Nothing but *deism* or *infidelity*. The only views held in common by the Jew, Mohammedan, Christian, and others are just those held by infidels. The religion of Odd-fellowship is *infidelity*, and its prayers are *infidel* prayers.

Not only such are the prayers and religion of Masonry and Odd-fellowship, but such *must* be the religion and prayers of all associations organized on their principles. The only way to welcome all of every creed, Jew, Mohammedan, Hindoo, etc., and make them feel at home in an association, is to exclude every thing offensive to the conscience or prejudices of any one of them. And when every thing of that sort has been excluded, the residuum, in every case, as every one must see, will be deism or infidelity. This is a serious matter. Christians are not free from guilt in countenancing such prayers and services. The tendency of such religious performances must be very injurious. Whoever adopts the religious, or rather irreligious, spirit and principles of Masonry, Odd-fellowship, and other similar associations must discard Christianity and the Bible. No doubt there are *some*, perhaps there are *many* Christians in connection with such associations, but they certainly do not and can not approve the Christless prayers of the lodge-room, much less join in them. Is it right for the disciples of Jesus, or even for believers in Christianity, as the great majority of people in this country are, to sustain any association which puts Christianity on a level with pagan superstition, which treats Jesus Christ with no more regard and veneration than it does Mohammed, Confucius, or Joe Smith, and whose only religion is the religion of infidels?

If secret associations did not pretend to have *any* religion or *any* religious services, but would, like bank and railroad companies, conduct their affairs without religious forms, it would be infinitely better.

CHAPTER V

Their Exclusiveness

1. Another objection which may be urged against secret societies in general, is their selfish exclusiveness.

It is well known that the Christian religion has often been subjected to reproach by the bigotry and sectarianism of its professors. If the *Bible* inculcated bigotry and sectarianism, it would be a well-founded objection to Christianity itself; but Christianity is eminently catholic and democratic, and is diametrically opposed to an exclusive and partisan spirit. The command of Christ to his church is to make no distinction on account of class or condition, but to receive all, and especially to care for the poor, the unfortunate, the oppressed, the blind, the lame, the maimed, and the diseased. Sometimes men calling themselves Christians act so directly contrary to the impartial, catholic spirit and teachings of Christ as to render themselves unworthy of all sympathy and encouragement; but the exclusiveness of secret societies is, we think, unparalleled in our day for its selfishness and meanness. They claim to be charitable and benevolent institutions; they assert that membership in them confers great honors and advantages; they profess (at least many of them) to act on the principle of the universal brotherhood of men and fatherhood of God. (Moore's Con.

of Freemasonry, p. 125; Webb's Monitor, pp. 21, 51; Proceedings of Odd-fellows' Grand Lodge of United States, 1859, App., p. 6.) We say nothing now about the falsity of these claims and professions; but we assert that, even admitting the boasted honors and advantages enjoyed by members of secret associations, such associations are eminently exclusive and selfish. Of this proposition there is abundant proof.

2. The Masons utterly refuse to admit as members women, slaves, persons not free-born, and persons having any maim, defect, or imperfection in their bodies; or, at least, the principles of Masonry forbid the admission of all such persons. (Masonic Constitutions, published by authority of the Grand Lodge of Ohio, Art. 3 and 4.) Moore, editor of the Masonic Review, in his Ancient Charges and Regulations of Freemasonry, in commenting on the articles above referred to, makes the following declarations: "The rituals and ceremonies of the order forbid the presence of women;" and "the law proclaiming her exclusion is as unrepealable as that of the Medes and Persians." (P. 145.) Again: "Masonry requires candidates for its honors to have been free by birth; no taint of slavery or dishonor must rest upon their origin." (P. 143.) Once more this author remarks: "A candidate for Masonry must be physically perfect. As under the Jewish economy no person who was maimed or defective in his physical organism, though of the tribe of Aaron, could enter upon the office of a priest, nor a physically defective animal be offered in sacrifice, so no man who is not 'perfect' in his bodily organization can legally be made a Mason. We have occasionally met with men having but one arm or one leg, who in that condition had been made Masons; and on one or two occasions we

have found those who were *totally blind* who had been admitted! This is so entirely illegal, so utterly at variance with a law which every Mason is bound to obey, that it seems almost incredible, yet it is true." (P. 152.) It is, hence, seen that Masonry is very exclusive. No woman can be a member. This regulation excludes at once one half of mankind from its boasted advantages. The oppressed slave is excluded; the man born in slavery, though now free, is excluded; the lame man is excluded; the man who has lost an eye is excluded; the man who has lost a hand is excluded; the man who has lost a foot is excluded; the man on whose birth any taint of dishonor rests is excluded; the man who is imperfect in body is excluded. No matter how good, patriotic, and wise such persons are, still they are excluded; no matter how needy such persons are, still they are excluded; no matter though a man have lost a hand, or foot, or eye in defense of his country and liberty, still he is excluded; no matter though a freedman, exhibiting bravery, and piety, and every virtue, still the "taint of slavery rests on his birth," he is excluded. Widows and orphans are excluded.

"If a brother should be a rebel against the state, the loyal brotherhood can not expel him from the lodge, and his relation to it remains indefeasible." (Moore's Constitutions, Art. 2.) A Mason may be engaged in a wicked rebellion, and may stain his soul and hands with innocent blood, and still he must be recognized as "a brother" and must continue to enjoy all the boasted rights and advantages of the order; but the patriot soldier who has been disabled for life in defense of his country and liberty is excluded. The widows and orphans of rebel Masons slain in battle, or righteously executed on the scaffold, must receive "the benefits;" but the widows and orphans of patriot soldiers who did not choose to join the Masons, or were excluded by some bodily imperfection, or by wounds received in battle, are left to the charities of "the ignorant and prejudiced." The Jew, the Turk, the Hindoo, the American savage, and the infidel (provided they are not atheists), are eligible to the boasted honors and advantages of Masonry. (Moore's Constitutions, pp. 119, 123.) But if a man have every intellectual gift and every moral virtue, and have some bodily imperfection, he is excluded. A man may be as gifted and as learned as Milton, as incorruptible and patriotic as Washington, and as benevolent as Howard, but if he is physically imperfect he is excluded from this association, which claims to be no respecter of persons, but to be the patron of merit, and which professes to act on the principle of the universal brotherhood of men.

3. Exclusiveness in about the same degree characterizes other secret societies. The Constitution of the Odd-fellows' Grand Lodge of Ohio provides that the candidate for membership must be "a free white person possessed of some known means of support and free from all infirmity or disease." (Art. 6, Sec. 1.) Substantially the same qualifications for membership are required by the constitutions and laws of other secret associations. (Constitution of Ancient Order of Good-fellows, Art. 6, Sec. 1; Constitution of Improved Order of Red Men, Art. 5, Sec. 1; Constitution of United Ancient Order of Druids, Art. 8, Sec. 1.)

4. Not only are these associations exclusive and selfish in regard to receiving members; not only do they utterly refuse to admit a man, however good, and wise, and

patriotic he may be, in case he is diseased or infirm, or is disabled by wounds in the service of his country, and is too poor and feeble to maintain himself and his family; not only do they exclude all such persons from membership and from the boasted privileges, and honors, and pecuniary benefits pertaining thereto, but also their regulations in regard to their internal affairs manifest an unchristian, anti-republican, exclusive, selfish spirit. For instance, Masons will not, and, indeed, according to their regulations, can not, bestow funeral honors upon deceased members who had not advanced to the third degree. Those of the first and second degree can not thus be honored. They are not entitled to funeral obsequies, nor are they allowed to attend a Masonic funeral procession. (Webb's Monitor, pp. 132-133.)

Again: Though Masonry makes professions of universal benevolence on the ground "that the radiant arch of Masonry spans the whole habitable globe;" though it declares that every true and worthy brother of the order, no matter what be his language, country, religion, creed, opinions, politics, or condition, is a legitimate object for the exercise of benevolence, (Masonic Constitutions, by Grand Lodge of Ohio, p. 80); still it is declared that "Master Masons only are entitled to Masonic burial or relief from the charity fund." (Masonic Constitutions by Grand Lodge of Ohio, p. 39.) The rulers of Masons can not be chosen from the members of the first or second degree. It is thus seen that the first two degrees serve as a sort of substratum on which the other degrees rest, and the "honors and benefits" are not intended for persons of the former.

The exclusiveness and selfishness of other secret

associations are also apparent from their regulations. As shown above, they exclude all diseased and infirm persons from membership, and of course from all the "benefits." They generally provide that, in case of sickness or disability, a member shall receive three dollars per week, and in case of the death of a member, the sum of thirty dollars shall be contributed toward defraying his funeral expenses. But all the associations making such regulations also provide that a member who is in "arrears for dues" shall receive no aid in case of sickness or disability; and in case of the death of a member who is "in arrears for dues" nothing shall be contributed to defray his funeral expenses, and his wife and children, however destitute they may be, can receive no aid. In such cases, the destitute widow and orphans must not look to "the *charitable* association" of which the departed husband and father was a member, but to outsiders—yes, to "prejudiced and ignorant" outsiders—for aid to bury his dead body with decency. Grosch says, "The philosopher's stone is found by the Odd-fellow in three words, *Pay in advance.* There are few old members of the order who can not relate some case of peculiar hardship caused by non-payment of dues. Some good but careless brother, who neglected this small item of duty until he was suddenly called out of this life, was found to be not beneficial, and his widow and orphans, when *most* in need, were left destitute of all *legal* claims on the funds he had for years been aiding to accumulate." (Monitor, p. 198, 199.) Such facts as these prove secret associations to be exclusive, heartless, selfish concerns. (See Constitution of Druids, Art. 2, Sec. 1, and By-laws, Art. 11, Sec. 1; Constitution of Good-fellows, Art. 16, Sec. 1; Constitution of Amer. Prot. Asso., Art. 9, Sec. 1-5.)

CHAPTER VI
False Claims

1. Another very serious objection to secret societies is that they set up false claims. No doubt a secret association may exist without doing so, but the setting up of false claims is the legitimate result and the usual accompaniment of secrecy. The object of secrecy is deception. When a man endeavors to conceal his business affairs, it is with the design of taking advantage of the ignorance of others. Napoleon once remarked, "The secret of majesty is mystery." This keen observer knew that the false claims of royalty would become contemptible but for the deception which kings and queens practice on mankind. We have quoted above from a book, the reliability of which will not be called in question, to show that the design of secrecy, on the part of Masons, is to take advantage of "a weakness in human nature," and to invest with a charm things which, if generally known, "would sink into disregard." So, also, "the aid of the mysterious" is resorted to by Odd-fellows to render their "meetings attractive," and to "stimulate applications for membership." (Proceedings of Grand Lodge, 1859, App., p. 10.) It will scarcely be disputed that such is the design of the concealment practiced by secret associations in general. It is thus shown that secrecy is the result of an unwillingness to rely upon real merit and the

sober judgment of mankind for success, and of a desire, on the part of associations practicing it, to pass for what they are not. Hence, the design of secrecy involves hypocrisy, or something very much like it.

2. But, whatever may be the *design* of secrecy, secret associations do set up false claims. They all, or almost all, claim to be charitable institutions. This is the frequent boast of Masons and Odd-fellows. Moore, in his "Constitutions," declares that "charity and hospitality are the distinguishing characteristics" of Masonry. (P. 71.) In the charge to a "Master Mason," at his initiation, it is declared that "Masonic charity is as broad as the mantle of heaven and co-extensive with the boundaries of the world." (Masonic Constitutions, published by the Grand Lodge of Ohio, p. 80.) "The Right Worthy Grand Representative," Boylston, in his oration delivered in New York, April 26, 1859, declared that Odd-fellowship is "most generally known and commended by its charities." (Proceedings of Grand Lodge, 1859, App., p. 6.) Such is the style in which secret associations glorify themselves. Such boasting, however, is not good. It is contrary to the command of our Savior: "Therefore, when thou doest thine alms, do not sound a trumpet before thee, as the hypocrites do in the synagogues and in the streets, that they may have glory of men." The boasting of secret associations about their charities is precisely what our Savior not only forbids, but also declares to be characteristic of hypocrites. And such boasting is, indeed, generally vain. When a man boasts of any thing, whether of his wealth, pedigree, bravery, wisdom, or honesty, there is good reason to suspect that his claims are not well founded. Hence, the very boasting of secret associations about their benevolence and charities is

37

presumptive evidence that their claims to the reputation of being charitable institutions are hypocritical and false.

3. In the first place, "the benefits" are confined to their own members. The excuse for secrecy, in some instances, is that it is necessary in order that aid may not be obtained by persons who are not members. In the "charge" delivered to a Master Mason at his initiation, he is enjoined to exercise benevolence toward "every true and worthy brother of the Order." In Boylston's address which we have already quoted from several times, "the well-earned glory of Odd-fellows" is declared to consist in this: that "no *worthy Odd-fellow* has ever sought aid and been refused." (Proceedings of Grand Lodge, 1859, App., p. 9.) It is provided in the Constitution of Odd-fellows, Good-fellows, etc., that aid shall be given to members under certain circumstances; but it will be in vain to search in them for any regulation providing for relief to any but members and their families. The provision found in the constitution or by-laws of almost every secret association that members "in arrears for dues" shall not be entitled to "benefits," plainly shows that their vaunted "charity" is restricted to their own members. This would not be so bad were it not for the fact that they carefully exclude from membership all who need aid or are likely to need aid. The Masons, according to their Constitutions, must not receive as a member any man who is not "physically perfect." The constitutions of other secret orders exclude all who are diseased or infirm in body, or who have no means of support. They exclude the blind, the lame, the maimed, the diseased, the destitute, the widow and the orphan, and all who are wretchedly poor or can not support themselves, and they cut off all such persons, together with their own members who "are in arrears,"

from the "benefits." Yet they talk about the universal brotherhood of men, and claim for themselves the possession of universal benevolence!

4. Still further: The relief afforded to members is not to be regarded as a charity. The amount granted in all cases is the same. The constitutions of most secret associations that give aid to members provide that three dollars a week shall be given in case of sickness, and thirty dollars in case of death. The amount given does not correspond to the condition of the recipient. The rich and the poor fare alike. The member "in arrears" is not entitled to any aid. It is only the *worthy brother* who is entitled to aid, and in order to be a worthy brother a member must punctually pay his "dues." Hence, the amount bestowed in case of the sickness or death of a member is to be regarded as a debt. The "Druids," in their Constitution, expressly declare that the aid given to sick members is not to be regarded in any other light than as the payment of a *debt*. "All money paid by the grove for the relief of sick members shall not be considered as charity, but as the just due of the sick." (Art. 2, Sec. 7.) Boylston, in his oration, though boasting of the "charities" of Odd-fellowship, declares that they do not wound or insult the pride of the receiver, for the reason "that the relief extended is not of grace, but of right." (Proceedings of Grand Lodge, 1859, Appendix, p. 6.) Grosch, in his Odd-fellows' Manual, in justifying equality in dues and in benefits, says: "He who did not pay an equivalent would feel degraded at receiving benefits— would feel that they were not his just due, but alms." (P. 66.) It is, hence, seen that the aid bestowed by secret societies is no more a gift of charity than the dividends of a bank or of a railroad company. The stockholders are

entitled to their share of the profits; so members of secret societies are entitled to a certain share of the funds to which they have contributed. We say nothing for or against the propriety of this arrangement, in itself considered. Persons have, perhaps, a right to form themselves into a mutual insurance company, to bargain with one another that they will aid each other in case of sickness or want; that in case of the death of any of the members, their families shall be provided for by the surviving members; that only the members who continue to pay into the common fund a certain sum monthly or quarterly shall receive such aid; that no money shall be paid out of the common fund for the benefit of any who are not members, or of their families; and that all diseased and infirm persons, and very poor people, such as "have no visible means of support," and are likely to need pecuniary aid, shall be excluded from the company and from its benefits. Perhaps men have a right to form themselves into an association with such regulations; perhaps they have a right to leave "an unworthy brother" (a member who fails to pay his "quarterly dues") and his family to the charities of "ignorant and prejudiced" people who will not join secret societies; and in case of the death of such a member, to leave his poor heart-broken widow to beg of the same "ignorant and prejudiced" outsiders enough of money to bury his dead body decently; *but they have no right to call themselves a charitable association*. It is probable that many Masons, Odd-fellows, Good-fellows, etc., are kind to "unworthy brethren," and to the poor in general; but if so, they are better than the associations of which they are members. Bankers and money-brokers, no doubt, sometimes show kindness to the poor, but it does not hence follow that banks and money-shaving establishments are charitable institutions. Neither does it follow that secret societies are charitable because their members, in case of sickness or death, are entitled to a certain portion of the funds which they themselves have contributed as initiation fees and quarterly dues, while those who are in real want can not even become members. What charity is there in persons pledging themselves to aid each other in sickness or other misfortune, and to let widows and orphans, the lame and the diseased, and the wretchedly poor, perish with hunger and cold? It may not be improper for A, B, and C to promise that they will take care of each other in sickness, and that in case of the death of one of them his dead body shall be buried by the survivors. It may, also, not be improper for a man to get his life or his property insured. Insurance companies have done much good. Many a man has been saved from pecuniary ruin by getting his property insured, and many a man has secured a competence for his wife and children by getting his life insured. Individuals and families have probably been oftener saved from worldly ruin by insurance companies than by secret societies. The association of A, B, and C may do some good. They have a right to agree to aid one another. They may, perhaps, have a right to say that D, E, and F, who are very poor, or are enfeebled by disease, shall not join them, and shall not be aided by them; but they have no right to represent their exclusive, selfish association as a charitable one. Such a representation would be false, and the wickedness of making it wholly inexcusable. We do not blame Odd-fellows, Good-fellows, Druids, or any other association for acting as mutual insurance companies. We do not blame them for agreeing that they will take care of each other or of each other's families. We are not now blaming them for excluding from their associations and from "the benefits" disbursed by them, the blind, the lame, the diseased, and the very poor who have no means of support, though this feature of such associations does seem very repulsive. We are not now condemning them for casting off all those who do not pay their "dues," those who become very poor and can not as well as the rich who will not, and for cutting off all such persons from all "benefits of whatsoever kind," though such treatment does seem to us selfish, cruel, and mean; we do not now arraign them for any of these things, however ungenerous, exclusive, and selfish they appear to us, but we do say that any association which thus practices, and professes, and calls itself a charitable one is a cheat and a sham. Those secret societies which glorify themselves on account of their charities and universal brotherhood and benevolence, can be acquitted of willful deceit and falsehood only on the ground that they are blinded by prejudice or ignorance, or both.

The pretentious character of secret associations appears, also, in their claims to be the possessors and disseminators of knowledge and morality. Their members seem to think a man can scarcely be good and intelligent without being "initiated." Webb delares "Masonry is a progressive science. * * Masonry includes within its circle almost every branch of polite learning." (Monitor, p. 53.) "Masonry is not only the most ancient, but the most moral institution that ever subsisted." (Monitor, p. 39.) Grosch, in his Manual, speaking of the shining sun as an emblem, says: "So Odd-fellowship is dispersing the mists from the advancing member's mind, and revealing things as they are; so, also, it is enlightening the world," etc. (Manual, p. 120.) The extravagance find absurdity of these claims must be evident to every prejudicial mind. It may be said, indeed, the above declarations express the opinions only of individuals, and that associations can not justly be charged with the errors of their members. We maintain, however, that secret societies are responsible for the vain boasting of their members. They claim that their members are a chosen board, a select few, who, by virtue of their association, are superior to the rest of mankind. Their processions and parades, their regalia and emblems, and their high-sounding titles are evidently designed to impress the minds of their own members and of outsiders with ideas of their excellence and grandeur. Their high-sounding titles have already been adverted to as involving the sin of profaneness; but they serve equally well to illustrate the pretentious character of the associations which employ them. Almost every officer among the Masons has some great title. There is the Grand Tyler, Grand Steward, Grand Treasurer, Grand Secretary, Grand Chaplain, and Grand Master. The Lodge itself is *grand*, and, of course, every thing and every body connected with it are *grand*. The treasurer, though his duty be merely to count and hold a little vile trash called money, is grand; almost every officer is a grand man.

These titles, however, do not give an adequate idea of the *grandeur* to which "sublime" Masonry ascends. They have their Right Worshipful Deputy Grand Master, their Right Worshipful Grand Treaurer , Most Worshipful Grand Master, Most Eminent Grand Commander, Thrice Illustrious Grand Puissant, Most Excellent Grand High Priest, etc. (Constitution of Grand Lodge of Ohio, Art. 5., Webb's Monitor, pp. 187, 219, 284.) Other associations employ similar titles; indeed, Masonry, as the oldest association, seems to have been copied after by the rest. The Odd-fellows have almost the same parades, shows, and titles as the Masons. They have their aprons, ribbons, rosettes, and drawn swords; and they endeavor, by these and other clap-trap means, to recommend their association as a grand affair. They, too, have their Right Worthy Grand Lodge, Most Worthy Grand Master, Right Worthy Grand Secretary, Right Worthy Grand Treasurer, Right Worthy Grand Chaplain, etc.

We think it strange that men of sense should employ such titles. They would be ridiculous even applied to the greatest and best man that ever lived. They are more ridiculous than the bombastic titles given to civil officers in barbarous countries. The Sublime Porte of Turkey is outdone in this respect by secret associations in the United States.

6.
The absurdity of these high-sounding titles and other puerilities is further seen from the character of those who compose the associations which employ them. They boast that they receive as members almost all sorts of men except atheists; that men of every religious sect and every nation meet in their lodges as loving brethren, and on a perfect equality; that they welcome the Jew, the Arab, the Chinaman, the American savage, the infidel, and the Christian, provided they be sound in body and be able to support themselves; yet the officers elected by the lodges or squads of such persons, Jews, Arabs, Chinamen, savages, infidels and Christians, become Most Eminent Grand Commanders, Thrice Illustrious Puissants, etc. Yea, since brotherhood and *equality* characterize these associations,

the Jew, the Arab, the Chinaman, and the infidel are eligible to any office, and may become Most Worshipful Grand Commanders and Most Excellent Grand High Priests.

All this is calculated to produce laughter and contempt; but such is not the design. The design of those who make use of these grand titles and other clap-trap things is to recommend their associations as an excellent and grand affair. The design itself, and the means employed for its accomplishment, must, certainly, be condemned by every unprejudiced Christian mind.

CONCLUSION

We have thus briefly stated the objectionable features of what are generally called secret societies. It is mainly to their secrecy, oaths, and promises, their profanation of holy things, their exclusiveness and their setting up of false claims, to which we object. These are the things objected to in the foregoing treatise. We have written without any feeling of unkindness, and we trust, also, without prejudice. We had intended to urge additional considerations to show the evil nature and tendency of secret societies; but we have been restrained by the fear of swelling our treatise beyond a proper size.

PART II

SHALL CHRISTIANS JOIN SECRET SOCIETIES?

"With charity for all and with malice toward none," we bring this question to all those who would serve Christ. We mean by "secret societies" not literary, scientific, or college associations, which merely use privacy as a screen against intrusion, but those affiliated and centralized "orders" spreading over the land, professing mysteries, practicing secret rites, binding by oaths, admitting by signs and pass-words, solemnly pledging their members to mutual protection, and commonly constructed in "degrees," each higher one imposing fresh fees, oaths, and obligations, and swearing the initiated to secrecy even from lower "degrees" in the same Order.

Shall Christians join societies of this kind?

SUPPOSING IT TO BE INNOCENT, WILL IT PAY?

First. They consume time and money. Have you considered how much? How many evenings, and whole nights, and parts of days? How many dollars in fees, dues, fines, expenses, and diminished proceeds from broken days? Will it pay? Can you not lay out this amount of time and money more profitably?—a plain man's question. They propose helping you to "friends," "business," in "moral reform," in "sickness, death, and bereavement;" but can you not get as much of such good in ways pointed out to you by Christ, your best and wisest friend?—ways which will yield you more of personal cultivation, spiritual good, earthly profit, social and domestic happiness, and openings for usefulness. If so, these orders are unprofitable, and *will not pay*.

Secondly. They furnish inferior security for investments. As *mutual insurance societies*, they are irresponsible, and more liable to corruption, *just because they are secret.* Do they make "reports" to the public or the Legislature? Do they make any adequate "report" to the mass even of their own members? Millions and millions are known to have gone into the treasury of a single one of these organizations. No dividends are declared, no expenditures published. *Where* is the money? Were it not safer to invest the same amount in companies where every proceeding is open to public eye and public judgment? Would you not, then, be safer? If so, *it will not pay* to join these orders.

IS IT OBLIGATORY?

First. Charity has no need of them. They are not truly charitable institutions. "Mutual insurance societies" they may be, though of an inferior sort, as we have seen; but that does not elevate them into *charitable* institutions. To bestow on your widow and orphans, your sickness, and funeral some pittance, or the whole of what you paid during health and life, is not *benevolence.*

But, further, it is well to ask, in determining how greatly

charity depends on them, how broadly they go forth among the poor outside their membership. During the anti-masonic excitement of 1826-1830 some two thousand lodges suspended. The resultant suffering was less, perhaps, than what would follow the suspension of a single soup association, any winter, in some city. Blot out the whole, and how small the injury to the charities of the country!

The Church of Christ is commanded to "do good unto *all* men"—"to remember the poor." It is engaged in this work. It blows no trumpet—it does not parade its charities; but it shrinks from comparison with no one of these orders, nor with all of them combined. *Christians* need not to go into them to preserve *charity* alive, or to find the best ways of exercising their own.

Secondly. Morality does not depend on them. We need say nothing of "what is done of them in secret." But, looking at what is open to all, we ask, What *work* are they doing worthy of so much organization, and expense, and time to reclaim the fallen, to banish vice, and to save its victim? We have heard them refusing him admission or cutting him off, but we have not heard of any considerable aid which they have given to public or private morality. And, further, do we not find them narrowing the circle of obligation, substituting attachment and duty to an order for love and obligations to mankind? *Membership* in a lodge, *not character*, is held to make one "worthy," opening the way to favor and society. But can all this be done without sensibly weakening the fundamental supports of morality, without lessening its broad requirements?

Thirdly. Patriotism has no need of them. They tend to destroy citizenship, to exalt love of an order above the love of country. The boast during the late rebellion was sometimes heard that their members, owing to the oaths of mutual protection, were safer among the rebels than other captives. Was the converse true? Were rebels, being Freemasons, safe or safer against restraint and due punishment when, falling captive to those of their order? How far does all this extend? To courts and suits at law? Are criminals as safe or safer before judge and jury of their order? Have rebellion and vice found greater security here? This boast is confession—confession that the ties of an order are stronger and more felt than is consistent with a proper love of country. Is justice thus to be imperiled? Are securities of property and rights thus to be imperiled? Must we beggar ourselves by paying fees and dues to one another of these orders, now becoming more plentiful every decade, to make sure of standing on equal footing and impartiality with others, in the courts and elsewhere, and imagine that all this is helpful to patriotism or even consistent with it?

Fourthly. Religion has no need of them. "The church is the pillar and ground of the truth." "The gates of hell shall not prevail against it." The preaching of Christ and him crucified is and must continue to be the wisdom of God and the power of God unto salvation. *Religion*, then, has no need of these secret orders.

We come now to this: Neither charity, morality, patriotism, nor religion imposes obligations on us to join them. *It will not pay* was our first fact. We have now reached this other, that *no consideration of duty* requires it. But,

IS IT RIGHT?

First. Christ, our Master, neither instituted nor countenanced these orders. Reviewing his whole earthly ministry, he said (John xviii: 20): "I spake openly to the world;" and "in secret have I said nothing." By this double affirmation he strongly suggested his preference for *open, unsecret* ways and proceedings.

Secondly. In those rites, proceedings, and regalia which do appear, these orders are frivolous, belittling, and unworthy of respect. If the revealed are such, what must the unrevealed be?

Thirdly. These orders stand convicted of deceit and falsehood. They profess secrets and mysteries worth buying. Hundreds of high-minded men, of irreproachable character and integrity, who have, therefore, "renounced these hidden things of dishonesty," testify over their own signatures, that their secrets are but signs, pass-words, ceremonies, etc., covering nothing but emptiness and vanity.

Fourthly. These orders are unfriendly to domestic happiness and well-being, breaking in upon the sacred confidence and unity of husband and wife, pledging him to conceal from her the proceedings of perhaps fifty nights yearly, thus often sowing seeds of distrust, filling his breast with what must not be divulged to her, involving him in affairs and habits not unfrequently injurious to the best interests and state of the family.

Fifthly. These orders are hostile to the heavenly-mindedness, the spirituality of those who join them. We speak from much testimony. "Let him that thinketh he standeth take heed." The prudent man foreseeth the evil, but the foolish pass on and are punished. This voice of one is that of many concurring wise, faithful, and godly men, viz.: "I am afraid of these secret societies; they have sucked the spirituality out of all the members in our church who have joined them." Young, promising Christians have often been blighted by them. The fervor of piety, interest in the church and its work, interest in Christ and his people, interest in God's Word and Spirit, all the various elements of an earnest life of faith and heavenly-mindedness have been blighted in these lodges. And in urging this, we appeal to so many witnesses, and cover so wide a field of observation, as to make it certain that this is not the exceptional but the ordinary result.

Sixthly. These orders tend to destroy Christian fellowship. Let them grow until a given church is broken into squads, each pledged to secrets from the other, but bound within itself by special ties; give to each its own weekly meeting, mysteries, rites, signs, grips, pass-words; let each be sworn to provide for, protect, shield, and love its own adherents above others, and is not "*church fellowship*" annihilated? Can the Spirit of Christ flow freely from member to member through such partitions? Is this "one body in Christ, and every one members one of another?"

Seventhly. These orders tend to subject the church to "the world" in some of its dearest interests. For example: When a few leading members join a neighboring lodge, and make vows to the "strange" brotherhood, how easy for that lodge to interfere secretly but controllingly in its discipline of members, or in its selection or dismission of a pastor! These suggestions are not merely imaginary. Subjection of the church, in this way, to the cunning craftiness of evil and designing men is no mere dream.

Eighthly. These orders dishonor Christ. Those claims which he makes for himself are disallowed. He is required to disappear or find a place amidst other objects for worship. There is a *necessity*, because these orders are designed for adherents of all religions. Were they on the footing of an insurance company or a merchants' exchange, or any similar body, this fact would not be so. But they profess to include religion among their elements, and its services, in whole or in part, among their ceremonies. They have prayers and solemn religious rites. And in these *Christ is dishonored.* His exclusive claims are disallowed or ignored, and this not by accident, but of set purpose. Out of twenty-three forms of prayer in the "New Masonic Trestle-Board," (Boston edition, 1850,) only one even alludes to him, and that one in a non-committal way. These secret orders are under bonds not to honor Christ as he claims, lest the Jew, or the Deist, or the Mohammedan, all of whom they seek to enroll in equal membership, should be offended. When the higher "degrees" of Masonry allude to Christ and Christianity, it is but as one amidst many equals. We repeat it: Did these orders stand on the same footing with mercantile or other bodies in this matter, this objection might go for nothing; but they do not. Unlike them, they profess to have religious services. Indeed, they often boast of their religiousness, and avow their full equality in this with the church of God itself! Yet, if you join them, their "constitutions" prohibit you acknowledging, in their boasted religious services, what Christ, your Lord, not only claims for himself, but commands you to give unto him: that glory which is due to his holy name. Are they, then, not *Anti-christ* in this thing? And can you, without sin, consent to it, or uphold institutions which forbid you and others, in religious services, to honor him as your God and Savior, and which thus place him on the same level with Zoroaster, Confucius, or Mohammed?

Ninthly. These orders—the things now alleged being true—impede the cause and kingdom of God, and are, therefore, hostile to the largest, best, and deepest interests of mankind. Recognizing this, churches, conferences, associations, synods, and many eminently godly men, living and dead, have put forth their solemn testimony against them. Great lawyers, like Samuel Dexter; great patriots and statesmen, like Adams, and Webster, and Everett; great communities, like the American people from 1826 to 1830, have united to declare them not only "wrong in their very principles," but "noxious to mankind." But many Christians, rising higher and standing on "a more sure word of prophecy," have discovered in them the enemies of the Gospel and of the cross of Christ. Following him, their great exemplar in philanthropy as in godliness, who did nothing in secret, they refuse to have fellowship with the unfruitful works of darkness, choosing rather to reprove them.

Shall Christians join secret societies?

Will it pay? Are they under obligation to do so? Fellow-disciple, brother man, have you doubt on these questions? If it will not pay; if you are under no obligation to do it; if you have any doubt of its rightfulness, it is most assuredly your duty to refuse any connection with them.

We have no wish to press our reasoning beyond just limits. We have sought to avoid extreme statements. We now ask you whether, in the light of what has been brought to view, the weight of argument is not against your joining these orders and lending them aid? Even should you be able to stand up against their tendency to lower your personal piety and injure your Christian character, have we not here one of those cases where many brothers are offended or made weak? The Lord Jesus has said, "Whoso offends one of these little [or weak] ones, it were better for him that a mill-stone were hanged about his neck and he were drowned in the depths of the sea." Will you, then, however safe yourself, be the means, by your example, of bringing weaker brethren into such dangers? "We, then, that are strong ought to bear the burdens of the weak, and not please ourselves." "It is good neither to eat flesh, nor to drink wine, nor to do any thing whereby thy brother stumbleth or is offended [caused to sin] or is made weak." These words are not ours; they are God's.

Christian disciple, decide this question of secret societies with candor, with solemn prayer, and with a purpose to please God.

PART III

REPORT TO
CONGREGATIONAL
ASSOCIATION OF ILLINOIS

A PAPER ADOPTED BY THE GENERAL ASSOCIATION OF ILLINOIS OF THE CONGREGATIONAL CHURCHES, AT THEIR MEETING IN OTTAWA, 1866

The topics committed to us involve the following points:

1. The moral character of secrecy. Is it an element of an invariable moral character? and, if so, what? and, if not, what are the decisive criteria of its character?

2. Associations or combinations involving secrecy. Are they of necessity right or wrong? If not, what are the decisive criteria?

3. Religious rites and worship in societies or organizations, open or secret. Are any kind allowable? and, if so, what?

CHAPTER I

Secrecy, Its character

A presumption against secrecy arises from the known fact that evil-doers of all kinds resort to secrecy. This is for two reasons: (1.) To avoid opposition and retribution; and, (2,) to avoid exposure to disgrace. The adulterer seeks secrecy; so do the thief and the counterfeiter; so do conspirators for evil ends.

Secrecy, whenever resorted to for evil ends, is wrong. But may it not be resorted to for good ends? and is it not recognized as often wise and right in the Word of God? We answer in the affirmative. There is a certain degree of reserve, or secrecy, that should invest every individual. Our whole range of thought and feeling ought not to be promiscuously made known. There is a degree of secrecy necessary in the order, social intercourse, and discipline of the family. There is secrecy needed in dealing with faults and sins. Christ adopts this principle in his discipline. He says, "Tell him his fault between him and thee alone. If he repents, conceal it." There are confidential communications for important ends, or for council.

Concealment may be used as a defense against enemies, as in the case of the spies of Joshua, or the messengers of David, or when Elisha hid himself by the brook Oherith, by

God's order. So God hides the good in his secret place and under his wings.

Secrecy is opposed to ostentation and love of human applause. Hence, alms and prayer are to be in secret. God also resorts to secrecy in an eminent degree. He hides himself. He dwells in thick darkness. It is his glory to conceal his designs. In part, this is inevitable by reason of his greatness; in part, he resorts to it of set purpose.

It is a special honor and blessing of the good that he discloses his secrets to them.

Secrecy, then, is not of necessity wrong. Its character depends upon the ends for which it is used, and the circumstances and spirit in which it is used. There is a secrecy of wisdom, love, and justice, as well as a secrecy of selfish, malevolent, and evil deeds.

CHAPTER II

Secret societies

Of these there may be two degrees.

1. Where not only the proceedings of the society are secret, but even the existence of such a society is concealed.

2. Where the existence is avowed, and the signs and proceedings only are secret.

In associations, secrecy may be resorted to in both these ways for evil ends. Men may combine in associated societies to prey on the community, and the existence of such societies be hidden. Counterfeiters, horse-thieves, burglars, may thus associate for wrong, in the deepest secrecy.

So, too, secret associations whose existence is avowed may combine for selfish ends, and in derogation of the common rights of the social system. They may defend their members, to the injury of justice, in our courts. They may interfere with the management of churches and societies. They may bring an influence of intimidation to bear on public men. They may disseminate false principles of religion and morals. They may co-operate for political ends, and to effect revolutions.

And yet it is no less true that, in certain circumstances, secret societies of both kinds may be resorted to for good ends.

Secret societies may be rightfully resorted to for common council and united action, in the fear of God and with prayer, in a very dangerous state of the body politic, to resist incumbent evils, and the existence of such societies not be disclosed, if the state of the case would thus give them greater power for good. So, as a defense against known disloyal secret organizations, secret loyal leagues were rightfully resorted to as a means of united and concentrated action against organized disloyalty. And if, in resisting moral evils, secrecy gives power and advantage in devising measures to resist vice and crime, it is not sinful to resort to it.

All boards of trust generally have secret sessions, and legislative bodies resort to secret sessions rightfully, if the state of affairs demands it. It will be seen that secrecy is justified and demanded by peculiar circumstances or obvious ends to be gained. The reason of the case, therefore, is against secrecy, and in favor of open action, where no such justification can be made out. It is the nature of truth and right to be open. All things tend to it. There is nothing covered or concealed that shall not finally be proclaimed.

On the other hand, if secrecy is resorted to without reason; if it is made the basis of false pretenses; if it assumes the existence of something that is not, then it is not defensible. If it involves a profession of information to be communicated, and influences for good to be exerted, that do not exist, then it is a species of intellectual swindling which admits of no defense. The sciences and arts, the Bible and nature, are open to all. So is the book of history. What new science, or art, or history, or religion is there for secret societies to disclose?

CHAPTER III

Religious rites or worship in societies, open or secret—are any allowable? and, if so, what?

In order to answer this question, we need to consider certain fundamental and vital principles of Christianity.

1. All men, as depraved and guilty, need regeneration and pardon through the intervention of Christ.

2. There is access to the true God only through Christ: "I am the way, and the truth, and the life. No man cometh unto the Father but through me."

3. "Whosoever denieth the Son, the same hath not the Father; but he that acknowledgeth the Son hath the Father also."

All Christian churches are based on these truths, and the center and culmination of their worship is this recognition of Christ in the Sacrament as the Lamb of God, who taketh away the sins of the world. Christ, too, is the center of the worship of heaven.

Hence, if Christians associate with others in worship, it can rightly be only on the ground that the worship centers in

Christ, and acknowledges him as Lord, to the glory of the Father.

Hence, if, for the sake of extending an organization, men are admitted of all religions—Pagans, Mohammedans, Deists, Jews—and if, for the sake of accommodating them with a common ground of union, Christ is ignored, and the God of nature or of creation is professedly worshiped, and morality inculcated solely on natural grounds, then such worship is not accepted by the real God and Father of the universe, for he looks on it as involving the rejection and dishonor, nay, the renewed crucifixion of his Son. As to Christ, he tolerates no neutrality. He who is not for him is against him. These principles do not involve the question of secrecy. They hold true of all societies, open or secret.

If, on such anti-Christian grounds, prayers are framed, rites established, and chaplains appointed, ignoring Christ and his intercession, God regards it as a mockery and an insult to himself and his church. In it is revealed the hatred of Satan to Christ. By it Christ is dethroned and Satan exalted.

These principles do not exclude worship and prayer from societies. In any societies, true worship in the name of Christ will be accepted.

Let us now apply these principles to the societies of Free Masonry, the modern mother of secret societies. Concerning these we hold it to be plain:

That they have neither science nor art to impart as a reward of membership. The time was when there was a society, or societies, of working masons, coming down from the old Roman empire, and extending through the middle ages.

These were societies of great power, and wrought great works. The cathedrals of the middle ages were each erected by such a corporation, and attest their skill and energy.

But these corporations of working masons have passed away, and Masonry is now, even in profession, only theoretical, and in fact, so far as this art is concerned, is not even this. It does not teach the theory of architecture. The transition took place in 1717, after a period of decline in the lodges of working masons. All pretences to a history back of this, or to any connection with Solomon or Hiram, are mere false pretences and delusion for effect. No art is taught and no science is communicated by the system.

Practical ends, then, alone remain; and, in fact, the founders of the system avowed "brotherly love, relief, and truth" as these ends. The cultivation of social intercourse is also avowed as an end by defenders of the system. But such ends as these furnish no good reasons for secrecy; nor is secrecy favorable to a wise and economical use of the income of such bodies for purposes of benevolence. An open and public acknowledgment of receipts and expenditures is needed as a safeguard against a dishonest and wasteful expenditure of funds.

Nor is this all. The secrecy of the order, taken in connection with the principle of hierarchal concentration, and with the administration of extra-judicial oaths of obedience and secrecy, renders it, as a system, liable to great abuses in the perversion of justice, in the overriding of national law, and the claims of patriotism.

But the most serious view of the case lies in the fact that it professes to rest on a religious basis, and to have religious temples, yet is avowedly based on a platform that ignores Christ and Christianity as supreme and essential to true allegiance to the real God of the universe. Its worship, therefore, taken as a system, is in rivalry to and in derogation of Christ and Christianity.

And, as a matter of fact, this and similar systems are by many regarded as a substitute for the church, or as superior to it. Moreover, devotion to them absorbs time and interest due to the church, and paralyzes Christians by association with worldly men, and by the malignant power of the spirit of the world.

This system, and those who imitate its hierarchal and centralizing organization, also give power to those hierarchal principles and systems against which Congregationalism has ever protested as corrupting and enslaving the church.

The system also cultivates a love of swelling titles, and of gaudy decorations and display in dress, that are hostile to the genius of our Constitution, and to true republican and Christian dignity and simplicity.

From this system other organizations have borrowed much, and some do not essentially differ from it in practical working.

Other organizations, however, for the ends of temperance reform, have adopted modes of organization, display in dress, and secret signs for the purposes of recognition and defense. The ends and proceedings of these temperance societies are so well known that it is often denied that they are secret societies; yet they do, avowedly for purposes of defense, resort to secrecy, and have imitated modes of dress and organization found in Masonry. And members of Masonic lodges declare that they involve, in fact, all the principles of Masonic organizations, and rely on them ultimately leading to their own order.

While we recognize the true devotion of the members of these societies to the cause of temperance, and acknowledge and commend their active efforts to resist the progress of one of the greatest evils of the age, we yet can not concede the wisdom or desirableness of a resort to principles and modes of action which tend to create a current toward other secret organizations not aiming at their ends, nor actuated by their spirit of temperance reform.

In conclusion, we respectfully present the Association the following principles foradoption :

Resolved, 1. That in dealing with secret organizations, this Association recognizes the need of a careful statement of principles and a wise discrimination of things that differ.

2. That there are some legitimate concealments of an organized character—such as the privacies of the family and business firms, the temporary concealment of public negotiations at critical stages, the occasional withdrawal of scandals which could only disturb and demoralize communities, and the secrecy of military combinations; nor are we prepared totally to condemn all private plans and arrangements between good and true citizens, in great emergencies, to resist the machinations of the wicked.

3. That organizations whose whole object and general method are well understood, and are known to be laudable and moral—such as associations for purely literary or reformatory purposes—are not to be sweepingly condemned by reason of a thin veil of secrecy covering their precise methods of procedure; yet we deem that outer veil of secrecy to be unwise and undesirable, inasmuch as it holds out needless temptations to deeds of darkness, and gives unnecessary countenance to other and unlawful combinations; and, whenever the act of membership involves an *unconditional* oath or promise of submission, adhesion, and concealment, under all circumstnces , that compact is a grave moral wrong.

4. That there are certain other wide-spread organizations— such as Freemasonry—which, we suppose, are in their nature hostile to good citizenship and true religion, because they exact initiatory oaths of blind compliance and concealment incompatible with the claims of equal justice toward man and a good conscience toward God; because they may easily, and sometimes have actually, become combinations against the due process of law and government; because, while claiming a religious character, they, in their rituals, deliberately withhold all recognition of Christ as their only Savior, and of Christianity as the only true religion; because, while they are, in fact, nothing but restricted partnerships or companies for mutual insurance and protection, they ostentatiously parade this characterless engagement as a substitute for brotherly love and true benevolence; because they bring good men in confidential relations to bad men; and because, while in theory, they supplant the church of Christ, they do also, in fact, largely tend to withdraw the sympathy and active zeal

of professing Christians from their respective churches. Against all connections with such associations we earnestly advise the members of our churches, and exhort them, "Be ye not unequally yoked together with unbelievers."

www.ingramcontent.com/pod-product-compliance
Lightning Source LLC
Chambersburg PA
CBHW022128280326
41933CB00007B/593